Jakob Schlafke

THE CATHEDRAL OF COLOGNE

106 COLOR ILLUSTRATIONS

BONECHI VERLAG STYRIA

Vertrieb
für Österreich
VERLAG STYRIA, A-8011 GRAZ, Schönaugasse 64

für die Bundesrepublik Deutschland
Lahn Verlag, Wiesbadener Straße 1
D-6250 Limburg/Lahn

ISBN 3 222 11275 4

© Copyright 1990 by
CASA EDITRICE BONECHI
Via dei Cairoli, 18b - FIRENZE
Telex 571323 CEB

*Printed in EEC by
Centro Stampa Editoriale Bonechi*

Photographs by
JAKOB SCHLAFKE

Translated by
BARBARA ROBERTS

INDEX

A LITTLE OF HISTORY

Every country has its distinctive monument—India has the Taj-Mahal, Cambodia has Anghor Wat, Egypt has the Pyramids, Greece has the Acropolis, France has the Eiffel Tower, Italy has St Peter's—Germany undoubtedly can claim the Cathedral of Cologne as its hallmark. Today, when ever-expanding cultural horizons have brought us way beyond the Seven Wonders of the Ancient World, the Cathedral of Cologne ranks as one of the best known and loved. This is the year that marks the centenary of its completion.

The Cathedral's origins are as old as those of Cologne itself wich was proclaimed a Roman city in 50 A. D. and given the name Colonia Claudia Ara Agrippinenasium (CCAA). Its historical background has been revealed by excavations undertaken since the war. In 1941 when an anti-airraid shelter was built in the southern end of the Cathedral the floor of a large dining-room in a Roman willa was discovered. It dated back to the second century A. D. and contained a brightly coloured mosaic depicting Dionysus, the Roman god of wine. The war reduced much of Cologne to a pile of rubble. A team of archaeologists led by Professor Doppenfeld and Professor Weyres, in charge of work on the Cathedral, set about carefully exploring the ground under the Cathedral. In 1961-1962 they discovered the walls of a Roman temple built about 80 A. D. in honour of Mercury Augustus and very similar to the small temple of Fortuna Virile in the Foro Boario in Rome.

In 1946 during earlier excavations the apse of the old Cathedral's choir was discovered. The Baptistery which stood on the side of the temple overlooking the Rhine was built in 450 and was discovered in 1866. Between 1958 and 1966 the architect, Weyres, erected the chapel in the crypt and the archbishops' tombs which have been open to the public since December 17th, 1978 the day of the death of Archbishop Cardinal Frings, a man dearly loved by the people. Further excavations have revealed even more. For instance today we know that in the building on the northeastern edge of the Roman city opposite the city-walls there was round the third century A. D. a Christian oratory. The episcopal church was erected in 313 when the Emporer Constantine guaranteed religious freedom to all Christians with the Edict of Milan. The church consisted of religious buildings 130m long and more than 20m wide. From the Hafenmarket (Port Market) on the Rhine the Baptistery was reached by a flight of steps about 40m long leading to the atrium which adjoined the episcopal church on the western side. As such it was similar to the old St Peter's and St Paul's, in Rome. Maternus, bishop of Cologne at that time took part in the Synodes of Rome in 313 and of Arles in 314. In 355 the Franks crossed over the Rhine and destroyed part of Cologne. It is impossible to tell what effect this had on the area surrounding the Cathedral. Around 392 the temple of Mercury Augustus was burnt down so that it was possible to straighten the atrium in front of the church.

By 460 Cologne had fallen into the hands of the Ripuary Franks who proceeded to establish their court there. Christianity spread and the baptism of King Clodoveo was decisive in consolidating the new religion. In 550 a small chapel stood in the middle of the atrium. It faced east and was dedicated to the Virgin Mary. It was here in 1959 that the tombs of a woman and a baby of royal blood were found. Their possessions can be seen today in the Diözesanmuseum.

Saint Vernanzio Fortunato, bishop of Poitiers and a poet, visited Cologne in 567. His hymns are still sung today. He praised Bishop Carenzio for the help he had given the poor and his interest in building construction which had resulted in doubling the Cathedral's area. The atrium had been enlarged to make room for the ever-increasing number of believers. This included the addition of a women's gallery as well. The building with two choirs increased in size to 85m in length and 22m in width. From the Marienchor (Our Lady's Choir) in the east a corridor 8m long led to a circular presbitery 4.5m in diameter where mass was celebrated according to rites still in use in the East today.

In 751 the Carolingians and King Pipin succeeded the Merovingians to the Frankish throne. Hildebold, a friend and adviser to Charlemagne (768-814), was Bishop of Cologne from 782 and Archbishop from 795 of a new ecclesiastical territory which stretched from Belgium to Hamburg. With the coronation of Charles as Roman Emperor of the German people the Cathedral grew once more. Before 818 after the initial enlargements which resulted in the construction of the western atrium the Cathedral of Cologne was demolished. It was replaced by a new building of monumental proportions the so-called "Cathedral of Hildebold" which was consecrated in 870. Its dimensions, 95m by 29m with its transept 41m long, made it one of the largest cathedrals of its time. The Hilinus' Manuscript written round the year 1000 and kept in the Cathedral's Treasure House tells us it was the third episcopal church to rise on the hill. Archaeological excavations have confirmed this statement.

Numerous art treasures of that period have survived including manuscripts to be found in the Cathedral's Library and sacred relics which were brought from Rome to Cologne mainly by Archbishop Bruno, the younger brother of Emporer Otto I. They include Gero's Crucifix and the Casket, said to have belonged to the Three Wise Men whose remains were brought from Milan to Cologne in 1164 by Archbishop von Dassel. The citizens of Cologne would not rest until a worthy resting place was found for these precious relics. So on April 13th 1248 the order was given for work to begin on the construction of the new cathedral. When it was known that work on the Sainte Chapelle in Paris, the new church built for the coronation of the French kings, had taken only three years to the day of consecration, on 25th April 1248 the citizens of Cologne hurriedly set to work. They began with the eastern choir which was burnt down to make room for the new building. However the fire got out of control and destroyed the whole Cathedral. Fortunately the Casket of the Three Wise Men was saved. The eastern part of the building was temporarily reconstructed until finally, on August 15th 1248 Konrad von Hochstaden laid the foundation stone for the new building. By 1261 work had progressed to the stage where the Archbishop's burial could take place in the Achsenkapelle and the Bibelfenster (Bible Window) was already in place. By 1265 mass was being celebrated in the lower section of the choir. By 1300 work on the buttresses was completed and on September 27th 1322 on occasion of a provincial synode the choir was solemnly consecrated by Archbishop Heinrich von Virneburg.

Owing to political unrest at the time work on the Cathedral proceeded slowly over the next two hundred years. The Petrusportal (Peter's Door) in the southern tower with its ornamental statues was finished in 1322 and is evidence of the close ties Cologne had with the Parler family and Bohemia. From 1448 to 1449 the two bells were installed, the Pretiosa weighing 11.2 tons and the Speciosa of 6 tons. In 1560 when the southern tower was 59m high all building activity ceased and the crane which rose above it became the symbol of Cologne up until 1869.

The French Revolution heralded in hard times for the Cathedral. With the arrival of the revolutionary troops the sacred building was turned into a storehouse for the army. In the winter of 1797 to 1798 the prisoners-of-war used the wooden furnishings from the nave and the transept as firewood. Yet even in those times of deep despair there arose a new wave of enthusiasm as personified in such men as George Forster, Friedrich von Schlegel, Joseph Görres and the Boisserée brothers. These men managed to rally the people to the Cathedral's cause. Then in 1814 after Napoleon's defeat in Russia they managed to convince Prince Frederick William to recommence the work which for so long had been suspended.

In 1821 the Archbishopric of Cologne which had been suppressed by Napoleon was reestablished and the Cathedral was once more restored to its former prominence. The Prussian state which had confiscated all church property financed the reconstruction of the Cathedral.

Schinkel and Zwirner, the new man in charge of work on the Cathedral, made the plans and when in 1840 Frederick William IV acceded to the throne work began once more. Many German companies joined together to form a fund, the Zentral Dombau Verein, for the reconstruction of the Cathedral. In 1842 on September 4th Archbishop Cardinal Johannes von Geissel and Frederick William IV laid the foundation stone which was the signal for work to begin. In 1863 the dividing-wall built in the fourteenth century between the nave and the choir was demolished. By 1869 the northern tower was the same height as the southern one and the old crane which for 300 years had been the symbol of the city was finally pulled down. Then on 15th October 1880 in the presence of Emperor William I the final stone on the rose—window in the southern tower was put in place. The 157m tower was ready and the Cathedral which had been 632 years in the making was finally completed!

The third period of building activity began after the Second World War. The Cathedral which is near the station was hit fourteen times from the air and by many incendiary bombs as well. Ten vaults from the central nave and the same number from the aisles were destroyed. However by 15th August 1948 on the seven-hundredth anniversary of the laying of the foundation stone, the Cathedral's architect from 1944 to 1972, W. Weyres had already completed work on the restoration of the choir and by 1956 religious rites were being celebrated in the western part of the building. At present the director of works, A. Wolff, and his sixty assistants are busy repairing the remaining damage caused by the war as well as that caused by atmospheric pollution which is eating away at the stone. It is reasonable to ask if the magnificent Cathedral, the pride of Cologne, will ever be seen without its scaffolding. The people of Cologne say: "the day the Cathedral is finished will mark the end of the world".

ROM AM DOM

Round 1968 a lot of construction work was undertaken in the vicinity of the Cathedral. It included the Underground between the station and the Cathedral, the building of the Römisch-Germanisches Museum (Roman-Germanic Museum) and the construction of a garage below the Cathedral Square. As a result it was necessary to move the Cathedral workshop to a new site. In 1969 the whole area around the Cathedral was turned into one big workshop and in the early months it was the scene of many important discoveries as archaeologists worked away full-time. Their findings were put on show at the "Rom am Dom" exhibition which was opened on 14th November 1970 and closed on 14th February 1971. Nowadays children play under the Roman arch of the northern door which can be seen as one drives into the underground garage. Most people are unaware that the Gospel speaks of a side door very similar to this one in the parable of the camel and the eye of the needle.

A few taps of the shovel and the Cathedral revealed all its secrets. There appeared a labyrinth of walls, pipes for drinking water and heating, drains, layers of clay and ashes and what is more in front of the main door a large well which can still be seen in the underground garage and which in the time of Hildebold's Cathedral was situated in the centre of the atrium. Many new discoveries were made including settlements from the centre of the Roman city dating back to the stone and iron ages. An uninterrupted record of human habitation was found piled layer upon layer dating back to the dark ages and the time of the Merovingians. A small Frankish chapel was discovered. In all a dearth of information came to light on the history of the building of the atrium

From Roman times, the side arch of the northern door.

Excavations on front of the western door, April 1969.

in the old Cathedral. Most of the new discoveries were of the Roman period and included a whole district of the one-time city together with its streets, and houses with their furnishings and frescos. The finding of a small fragment confirmed that the 19th legion which together with the 17th and 18th was wiped out in the forests of Teutonburg along with the Roman consul Varo, had been encamoed in Cologne.

In the course of excavations for the Cathedral's new workshop in 1969 more mosaic floors of different styles came to light. One of them consisted of swastikas surrounded by a geometric design. It was part of a long passage-way which led to the temple of Mercury Augustus. A Frenchman, an expert in this field carefully removed the mosaic and part of it can be seen today in the Römisch-Germanisches Museum. The swastikas are evidence of the conflict between Christianity and the pagan cult of Mithra which lived on mainly among the Roman soldiers and veterans conscripted in the Middle East. In the course of excavations near the Cathedral two temples dedicated to her were discovered. One of them was reconstructed for the "Rom am Dom" exhibition so that visitors could appreciate the narrow aisles with their twelve seats, and the apse with the figure of Mithra. In the third century the conflict between the pagan cult of Mithra and Christianity became more bitter. It was in this period that work on the episcopal church began. In 1866 the Cathedral's architect, Voigtel, uncovered the Baptistery and undertook work to consolidate it. Today we can admire it through the gates on the eastern side of the Cathedral near the Dyonisosbrunnen (the Fountain of Dionysus). The star-shaped basin in the Baptistery dates back to the first half of the fifth century and

Archaeological finds.

Baptismal font (first half of the 5th century A.D.).

The Cathedral of Hildebold (818-1248).

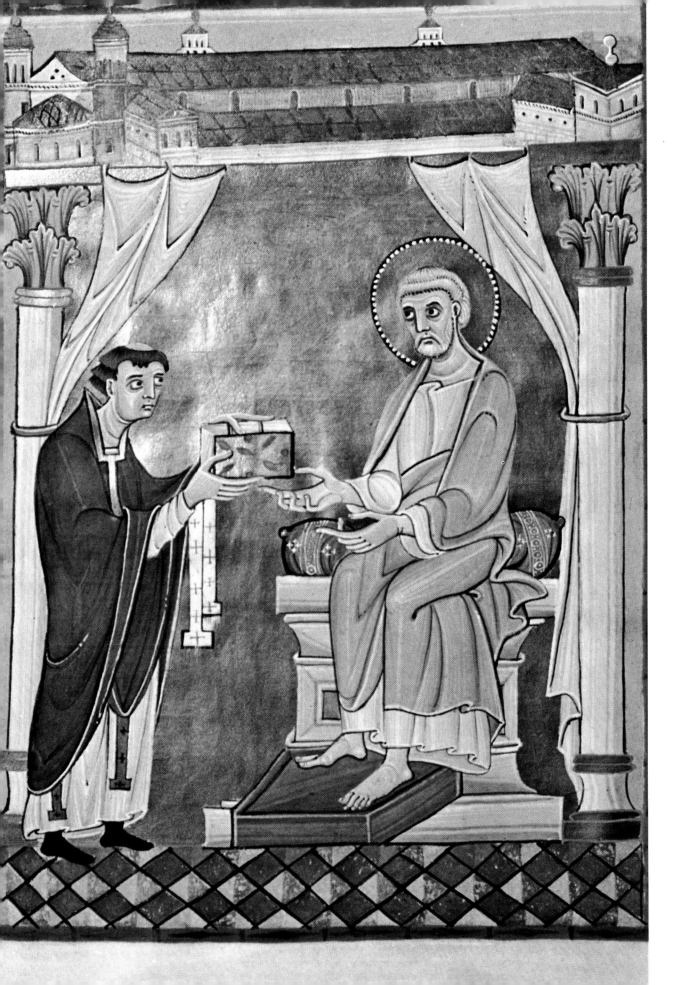

Gero's Crucifix (976).

Gero's Crucifix: Head of Christ.

replaces a preexisting one. It is in the form of an eight-pointed star, 4.7m. in diameter, and most likely there were columns on the tip of each point which may have supported a canopy. The inside of the fountain is 2m. wide and during the baptismal ceremony it was crossed in a north-south direction. The area surrounding the basin was in the form of a Greek cross and this was of symbolic significance. Mosaic tiles found in the vicinity, among which the blue ones stand out, lead us to believe that this Baptistery was very similar to the Mausoleum of Galla Placidia in Ravenna built round about the same time. It was probably already standing round the time of the Carolingians.

THE CATHEDRAL OF HILDEBOLD

One of the most precious manuscripts in the library of the Cathedral of Cologne is Hilinus' Manuscript, written for the consecration of Saint Eribertus who entered the city barefoot on Christmas night in 999. At his consecration the book of the Gospels was placed on his shoulders as a sign of the great responsibility his position demanded. On the dedication page of the manuscript reproduced here is the oldest drawing of the Romanesque Cathedral which lasted until 1248 when work on the construction of the Cathedral as we know it today began.

One of the most moving testimonies of that period is *Gero's Crucifix.* It was Archbishop Gero who in 971 went to Constantinople on behalf of Emporer Otto I to ask for the hand of Princess Theophany in marriage for Otto II.

Gero's huge Crucifix depicts Christ just after his death and is one of the largest crucifixes in the Western world. At present it hangs over the bishops' tombs near the entrance to the Sakramentskapelle.

As well as this work of art of the Cathedral of Hildebold there are in the Cathedral Treasure House many other precious objects including three links from the chain which bound St Peter in Rome and Jerusalem. It is preserved in a shrine from the fifteenth century. They

*The Shrine of the
Cross (11th-12th century).*

*The Ostensory-Shrine with three links
from St Peter's chain.*

*The Crucifix of Limoges
(12th-13th century).*

were brought to Cologne from
Rome during the time of Archbishop Bruno I (953-965).
Some of the Crusaders brought back
as precious relics from Jerusalem
fragments of Christ's Holy Cross.
The *Kölner Kreuzreliquiar* (Shrine
of the Cross of Cologne) where
they are kept was incorporated in
the 13th century into a triptych, a
Byzantine work of the 11th century
and a present from the Emperor
Alexis I of Constantinople.
Among other works of the twelfth
century is the *Prozessionskreuz*
(Crucifix of the Procession). The
body of Christ and the enamel
work was done at Limoges and
the rest was added in the thirteenth
century.

The Casket of the Three Wise Men on the Cathedral's High Altar (1180-1230).

The Casket of the Three Wise Men

In 1164 Archbishop Reinald von Dassel brought the remains of the Three Wise Men to Cologne from Milan where they had been kept up until then in an antique marble sarcophagus. The citizens of Cologne wanted to have a casket made of gold, silver and precious stones to hold such an important relic. The task was assigned to Nikolaus de Verdun, one of the most famous craftsmen of his time. In 1180 he arrived from Vienna with his team of craftsmen. By 1190 work was well under way. However forty years were to pass before the casket was finished. As it was the time of the Crusades and many treasures of antiquity were finding their way to the West some of them were used to decorate the casket.

The casket was in the form of a basilica with a nave and single aisles. It was 1.53m. high, 2.20m. long and 1.10m. wide. As the Three Wise Men became a symbol for all those who set out in search of God, Cologne was to become one of the greatest centres of pilgrimage in the Christian world, and the most frequented after Jerusalem, Rome, Santiago de Compostela and Aix-la-Chapelle. Even the German kings themselves after their coro-

nations at Aix-la-Chapelle went to Cologne to pay homage to Our Lord and offer him gifts as the Three Wise Men had done.

The casket shows the way in which God revealed himself to all peoples throughout time: to the pagan people through the wonders of nature and the star that guided the Three Wise Men, to the Jewish people through the words of the Prophets who can be seen on the lower part of the casket. On the sides of the upper section the Apostles can be seen.

The back part with the *Flagellation* and the *Crucifixion* on the two lower panels shows how the Lord with his suffering atoned for the sins of the world. The upper panel shows how the faithful gathered round him.

Today doubts are often expressed as to the authenticity of these relics and this is of course understandable. The early history of the Church, and, in particular, the first three centuries after Christ, is somewhat obscure because the early Christians had no churches in which to meet but were forced to gather in the catacombs to escape religious persecution. However the latest research carried out in 1979 dates the material in which bones were wrapped as being of the second to fourth century A. D. This is further proof of their authenticity. Such relics were greatly revered in the pre-Christian era. The story of the Three Wise Men is one of the most frequently recurring ones in the first four centuries of Christianity.

Front section: the Adoration of the Three Wise Men.

Upper panel of the front section: Christ Judging the World.

Upper section: Left Side, so-called "Solomon's Side": Cherub.

Ezekiel, the Prophet.

Moses.

Enamel ornaments with precious stones and trapezoidal piastres from classical times.

The Cathedral seen from the east.

THE GOTHIC CATHEDRAL

The relics of the Three Wise Men were among the most famous ever brought to Cologne and when the Casket was finished in 1230 it was decided that a new Cathedral of gigantic proportions should be built. Work on it began in 1248.

However a fire lit to demolish the eastern choir of the old Cathedral got out of control and the flames spread destroying the whole building. The western wing was temporarily reconstructed and in August of the same year the foundation stone for the new building was laid by Archbishop Konrad von Hochstaden. The seven chapels in the ambulatory and all of the

☐ 13th century

▨ 14th century

▨ 15th century

▨ 16th century

☐ 19th and 20th century

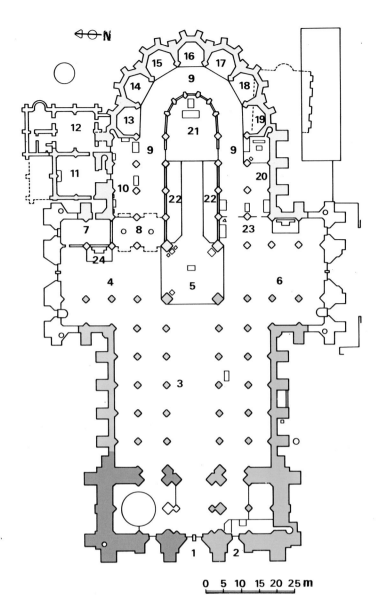

0 5 10 15 20 25 m

ground floor were designed by the Cathedral's first architect, Gerhard, and were completed by his successor, Konrad, after 1261. In 1265 religious rites were already being celebrated there. By the beginning of the next century the new choir with its system of buttresses was ready for use and seen from the Rhine it resembled a huge crown resting on the city's skyline. The most striking feature of the building was not so much its Gothic style of which there were already many famous examples in England and France but rather its huge dimensions. The Cathedral's exterior once finished was to have been 144m. long with a transept 86m. wide and a nave 15.5m. long and 61.5m. high. The inside was to have been 136.5m. long, 75.2m.

wide and 43.5m. high with aisles 19m. high. Plans made for the façade in 1296 forsaw the towers at their present height of 157m. The inside area of the Gothic Cathedral was to have been 6,166sq.m. which would have made it the largest church in the Christian world. However 632 years were to pass before this was to be realised! At the Provincial Synode of 1322 Archbishop Heinrich von Virneburg was only able to consecrate the choir but it was already as richly decorated then as it is today. The Casket of the Three Wise Men was to have been placed in the centre of the transept's cross but remained instead in the Marienkapelle, on the choir's central axis right up until the time of the French Revolution.

In the central stained-glass window in the upper section of the choir-stalls standing 17m. high is *The Adoration of the Three Wise Men*. Above it in nine double panels are the *Kings and Prophets of the Old Testament*. In the side windows of the upper section can be seen the *Twenty-Four Kings and Elders*. The delicate ribs between the windows support the ceiling vaults and resemble poles holding up a huge tent. The stained-glass windows of the Cathedral of Cologne in which green predominates over blue and red, in contrast to French cathedrals, inspire a sense of joy. On sunny mornings they shine like candles high up in the nave supported by their slender pillars. On the pillars' octagonal corbels brightly coloured statues of the *Apostles* can be seen as they walk towards Christ and the Virgin Mary carrying the symbols of Christ's Passion. Twelve angels playing musical instruments encircle the figures which stand 5m. high above the canopies. These statues are among the most beautiful in German Gothic art.

Beneath them the dividing-walls of the choir-stalls protect the faithful from the cold. The partitions are each 5.6m. long and 2.84m. wide. Their six surfaces contain a series of frescos finished in 1330. They begin with *The Life of Mary* from her birth to her coronation in

The western façade of the Cathedral.

The nave and the choir.

18

The choir-stalls.

The vaults from the choir-stalls.

Heaven. The main fresco depicts *Christmas Night*. It is followed on the southern side in a westerly direction by the *Legend of the Three Wise Men* which ends with the arrival of their remains in Cologne. The final panel is of the *Lives of Saint Felix, Saint Naborio, and Saint Gregory of Spoleto* whose bones lie in the casket with those of the Three Wise Men. Turning to the northern side and the eastern panel is the *Life of St Peter* from his early vocation with his brother Andrew to his martyrdom with St Paul. On the two remaining partitions is the *Life of Pope Sylvester* up until his meeting with the Emperer Constantine who gave him the Papal States in fiefdom. Beneath these grandiose frescos framed in Gothic architecture are to be found on the southern side the *Roman Emperors,* from Caesar right up until the German emperors of the Holy Roman Empire. On the northern side can be seen the Bishops of Cologne from Maternus to Archbishop Hermann von Hessen. This series of frescos is among the best preserved of the fourteenth century because after 1688 the dividing-walls were covered with tapestries by Rubens and Ramboux (19th century).

In the background of these large frescos the artist has painted tiny details of everyday life. These are similar to carvings on the choir-stalls whose 104 seats make them the largest in Germany. There are over 500 carvings on the stalls which include scenes of children playing and schoolboys' pranks, human passion, teaching, art and scenes from the building of the Cathedral itself and the casting of the bells. The choir-stalls in their fourteenth century form have special functions. The seats show us man's natural tendencies towards good and evil. The partitions remind us of how God will choose those few elect to save the world. The

Mary.

Christ.

James, the apostle.

Matthew, the apostle.

Angel with bag-pipes.
Angel with guitar.
Angel with violin.
Angel with drum.

The stalls and the dividing-walls of the choir.

figures on the pillars invite man after the trials and tribulations of this life to that heavenly paradise in the sky.

In the centre of the choir is the *Altar* which rests on the solid foundation of the hill on which the Cathedral is built. It is 4.52m. long and 2.12m. wide and one of the largest altars in the Christian world. White marble figures set in black marble slabs depict in four scenes the *Life of Mary:* the *Annunciation,* the *Visit of the Three Wise Men* and *Christ's Presentation at the Temple*. On the other side of the altar can be seen *Christ's Entry into Heaven*. The Apostles, Saints and Prophets surround these scenes. In the seven side chapels which surround the choir are buried many of Cologne's archbishops some of

Samson and the Lion.

Samson and Delilah.

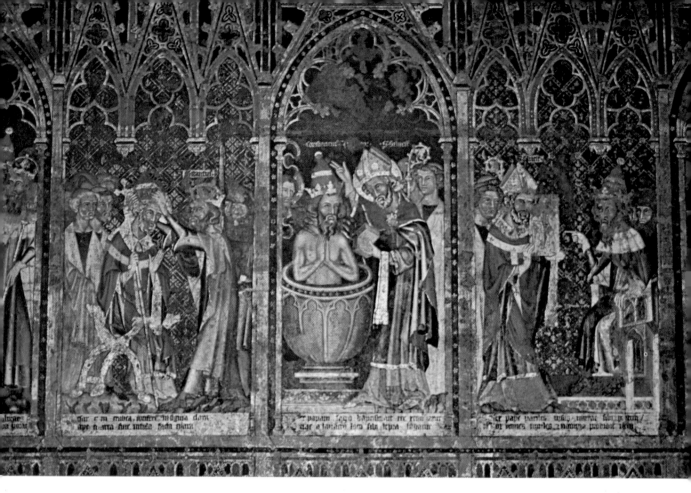

Dividing-walls in the choir: the Legend of St. Sylvester.

Angels playing musical instruments.

First Bible Window (1260) in the Dreikönigskapelle:
The Feast of the Pasha — The Last Supper.
Noah's Ark — The Baptism of Christ.
The Sacrifice of Samuel — Jesus' Presentation at the Temple.

*First Bible Window (1260)
in the Dreikönigskapelle:
The Adoration of the Three Wise Men.*

whose remains had been transferred here from the old Cathedral. The first one to be buried here was Archbishop Gero in 976. The imposing crucifix which bears his name was at first hung over his tomb but later was used as the sepulchral cross for all the tombs in the ambulatory and under the choir.

Several very valuable stained-glass windows from the second half of the thirteenth century have survived. The oldest made in 1260 and found in the Dreikönigskapelle (Chapel of the Three Wise Men) shows in twenty scenes the *Promise of the Old Testament,* the *Fulfillment of the New Testament* from the *Creation of Eve* and the *Birth of Mary* to *Christ's Ascension into Heaven.*

Second Bible Window (1280)
in the Stephanuskapelle:
The Annunciation of Mary.

Second Bible Window (1280)
in the Stephanuskapelle:
The Last Supper.

The Ambulatory

The seven chapels in the ambulatory were the first parts of the Gothic Cathedral to be completed. Their decorations belong to different periods, however. They are all burial chapels and keep alive the memory of the bishops who led the church of Cologne: opposite Gero's Crucifix Archbishop Wilhelm von Gennep (1349-1362) is buried; next to him in the Engelbertkapelle lies Archbishop Anton von Schaumburg (1556-1558); in the Maternuskapelle, opposite the Kreuzigungsaltar (Triptych of the Crucifixion), is Archbishop Philipp von Heinsberg (1167-1191) who extended Cologne's territory and enclosed it within citywalls. In the next chapel, the Johanneskapelle, Archbishop Konrad von Hochstaden (1238-1261) is buried. He lay the foundation stone for the Gothic Cathedral. This chapel also includes the very simple *Tomb of the Blessed Richeza,* queen of Poland, granddaughter of Emperor Otto II and sister of Archbishop Herman II of Cologne. La Marienkapelle in the axis of the Cathedral was known as the Dreikönigskapelle up until the beginning of the nineteenth century and it was here that the Archbisops of Cologne and the most important members of the Wittelsbach family (1583-1761) had their sepulchres built. Opposite these sepulchres today, behind the Casket of the Three Wise Men stands the *Tomb of Archbishop Dietrich von Moers* (1414-1463). The sarcophagus in the adjacent chapel, the Agneskapelle, houses the *Relics of Saint Irmgarda of Süchteln* (Aspel, 1085) who founded the hospital not far from the Cathedral.

The Michaelskapelle contains the sepulchre of *Archbishop Walram von Jülich* (1332-1349) and the Stephanuskapelle that of *Archbishop Gero* (969-976) whose tombstone in white marble with a red and green porphyry mosaic dates back to the time of the old Cathedral. Gero's Crucifix originally hung over the altar in this chapel opposite his tomb. In the same chapel we can admire the second of the pre-

The Ambulatory.

cious Bibelfensters (Bible Windows) dating back to 1280. It came from the Dominikanerkirche which was situated on the spot where the Post Office now stands. It was donated to the church by St Albert Magne and the then Archbishop, Siegfried von Westerburg. This precious work of art recalls how Albert Magne one of the most famous scholars of his time lived and taught in Cologne for many years and also played a great part in the religious concept of the Gothic Cathedral's construction and decoration. The stained-glass window consisting of eleven brightly coloured double panels relates the *Story of Salvation* and like the other Bible Window compares events from the

The stained-glass window of the Three Wise Men in the upper section of the choir-stalls.

Promise of the Old Testament with the *Fulfillment of the New Testament*. The chapels surrounding the choir, resplendent with their frescos and stained-glass windows, are among the Cathedral's most treasured works of art.

The Madonna of Füssenich
(end of the thirteenth century)

The eastern section of the Cathedral was from earliest times dedicated to Mary, mother of God. The chapel in the atrium of the old episcopal church of 550 already bore her name. In the present Cathedral there are over two hundred representations of her. Over the centuries, as Novalis expresses it in his verse, she has been of the utmost importance: "I can see

Madonna of Milan (without crown).

Enthroned Madonna (end of the 13th century) in the Dreikönigskapelle.

Madonna of Milan (with crown).

you, in a thousand works of love but not one of them portrays you as my soul sees you". Round about the fourteenth century numerous Madonnas were made similar to this one which Canon Alexander Schnütgen, an expert in Rheinish art, donated to the church in 1908 on the condition that it stand in exactly this spot on the Cathedral's axis. Mary, whose duty it was to make up for the ills of the world caused by Eve, holds an apple in her right hand and Jesus in her left while with her left foot she crushes a dragon. Her upright pose gives her an air of stern self-control while her candid eyes express a beauty which inspires courage. She seems to be saying that the Saviour who is Lord and master holds the world in the palm of his hand and is the source of all wisdom.

The Madonna of Milan

The Madonna on the central pillar of the Sakramentskapelle is one of the most noteworthy in the Cathedral. The crown, sceptre and halo of stars which were added in the nineteenth century spoiled somewhat the original beauty of the carved walnut figure which stands I.75m high. The additions were made in 1854 after the proclamation of the Dogma of the Immaculate Conception. In 1978 when the Sakramentskapelle was being reconstructed the Madonna was without her crown and hous-

ed in the Agneskapelle it was possible to admire her in all her former glory. Her resemblance to the Madonna on the pillar in the choir was once more evident which leads us to believe that they are both the work of Maestro Arnold who was in charge of the Cathedral's workshops from 1260-1295. This sculpture is one of the oldest from the Gothic Cathedral and it has the typical beauty of Rheinish art. The name, Madonna of Milan, is a reminder of the figure Reinald von Dassel brought with him from Milan along with the relics of the Three Wise Men in 1194. The Sakramentskapelle is considered one of the best examples of late Gothic architecture in existence. It was consecrated by Albert Magne in 1277.

33

The Western Façade

As soon as the choir was finished round 1300 work began immediately on the south-western tower. The façade which is 7,000 sq.m. in area is the largest church façade ever built. It was designed before 1300. Some of its plans were found in 1814 and 1816 in Darmstadt and Paris. By 1410 only the second floor of the southern tower was finished. The two aisles in the southern section reached a height of 14m. They were reached through the southern door which was built between 1370 and 1400 during the time of the Parler family. It was the only door to be completed during the Middle Ages.

The doors of the Gothic Cathedral were designed by the Cathedral's architects in collaboration with noted theologians of the time. They depict scenes from the Story of Salvation beginning with the creation of the world and ending with the Day of Judgment. The same was true for the Doors of Cologne which because of their great size were richly decorated. The middle door is 28m. high and depicts the *Story of Salvation* from the creation of the angels and the planets to the handing down of the law in the Sermon on the Mount. One by one all the great figures of the Old Testament appear. Mary takes pride of place in the centre of the door while Christ in the process of judging the world towers above them in the spires.

The Petrusportal
(Peter's Door)

Up until the Parler Exhibition in 1978 the Petrusportal had its original decorations.

In the tympanum, as in the northern section of the dividing-walls of the eastern choir-stalls, we can see the *Legend of Simon:* Simon the sorcerer in an attempt to prove his

Western door (19th century).

Paul and John from the Petrusportal.

Petrusportal (Peter's Door).

Apostles from the Petrusportal, today in the Diözesanmuseum.

The « Beautiful Madonna » (end of the 14th century) today in the Diözesanmuseum.

divinity soars through the air. Peter however sees him and exorcizes him. Simon falls down to earth dead. The lower panel shows *Nero Condemning Peter and Paul to Death*, one by crucifixion and the other by the sword. Of the statues in the jambs the five inside ones were the originals but are now to be found in the Diözesanmuseum. They show the two lots of brothers, *Peter and Andrew, Jacob and John,* and *Paul.* The most carefully worked statues are those of Peter, Paul and John who were chosen to preach the Gospel. They are seen in subtly distinguished periods of their life, Peter as an old man, Paul as an adult and John as a lad. On the inside arch there are the *Six Prophets,* on the second one to the side the *Four Evangelists* and on the other one the *Four Great Masters of the Western Church.* On the third arch to one side are *Sts. Catherine, Barbara, Dorothy, Helen* and *Elizabeth* and on the other *Sts. George, Stephen, Lawrence, Nicholas* and *Quirinus.* On the outside arch can be seen the *Archangels Michael* and *Gabriel* each surrounded by a Patriarch and angels playing musical instruments. The figures are seated on Gothic thrones richly adorned with fretwork a reminder of the close ties that existed between Prague and Cologne.

The "Beautiful Madonna"
(beginning of the 15th century)

At the 1978 Parler Exhibition of the statues from the southern door there was one which up until then was to be found in the south-aisle on the pillar in front of St. Christopher. The sculpture in stone stands 99cm high and is a work typical of the delicate Rheinish art of the early fifteenth century. It can be found today in the Diözesanmuseum.

The Altarpiece of St. Clare

In addition to those works commissioned especially for the Cathedral there are many others that found their way there at the end of the Napoleonic era. Among such works is the *Klarenaltar* (the Altarpiece of St. Clare) which originally came from the Convent of St. Clare near the Roman Tower. When the convent church was demolished in 1804 the altarpiece was rescued by Professor Wallraff and S. Boisereé and later donated to the Cathedral in 1811. Up until 1894 it was housed in the Johanneskapelle and then moved to the refectory behind the altar in the choir. Since the war many attempts have been made to restore it but it seems that only inside the Cathedral is the air suited to this delicate work of restoration. With this in mind a laboratory was set up in the choir itself and at present work on the altarpiece is near completion. It is hoped to be on view to the public once more in 1980. The Klarenaltar is 3.35m. long and 2.85m. high. It has two side sections. At the top are the *Twelve Apostles* and below *Twelve Shrines to the Saints* in the form of busts. The paintings were finished in 1360 but were later added to. The oldest style is typical of the school of Cologne at that time. The figures are slender and supple and recall the graceful lines of works of the first half of the fifteenth century. Some of them are accredited to the legendary master, Wilhelm von Heerle, the most famous artist of his time.

The paintings in the upper section tell the *Story of Christ's Passion* up until his resurrection and ascension into Heaven. His descent into Limbo is also depicted as in the case of the Passionsbalken (Passion Beam). Lower down is the *Story*

The Sepulchre of Archbishop
Wilhelm von Gennep (1362).

« Passionsbalken » (the Passion
Beam): the Deposition.

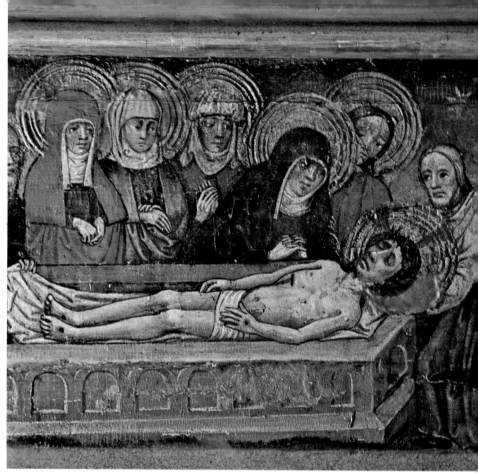

The Descent of Christ into Limbo.

of Christ's Childhood, from the
Annunciation to his presentation
at the temple in his twelfth year.
In the photo reproduced here we
can admire the delicate refinement
of the figures of Mary and the
angels in the Annunciation scene.
Their incorporeal subtlety accen-
tuates the respect and humility con-
veyed by their expressions and
gestures.

The Cathedral as the Archbishops'
Sepulchral Church

Sepulchre of Archbishop Wilhelm
von Gennep who died in 1362.
Above the Passionsbalken (Passion
Beam) 15th century; the Kreuz-
altar (Altarpiece of the Crucifix-
on) 1683 and Gero's Crucifix of 976.

The Kreuzkapelle
(The Chapel of the Cross)

The Kreuzkapelle is named after Gero's Crucifix. No other part of the Cathedral is as suggestive as the Kreuzkapelle. Gero's impressive Crucifix with the majestic immobility of the dead Christ cannot fail to inspire a state of deep meditation. The entrance to the chapel contains the epitaph of the architect, Konrad Kuyn (1445-1469) who asks for St Peter's intercession on his behalf to the Virgin Mary. The *Tomb of Archbishop Engelbert III* who died in 1368 and the supine *Statue of St Engelbert I* (d. 1225) may give the visitor to the ambulatory the impression of being in a mausoleum.

However these chapels do not speak only of death but also of eternal life: the late-Gothic "Passion Beam" (15th century) with its bright colours is a good example of this. It stands above the sepulchre of Archbishop Wilhelm von Gennep and depicts in twelve scenes *The Way to the Cross*. However it ends with the Resurrection and the final liberation from the chains of death and the devil.

Saint Christopher

One of the most famous statues in the Cathedral of Cologne is an enormous one of St Christopher. It stands 3.73m high and dominates the entrance to the southern part of the ambulatory. It is the work of a sculptor known as "Maestro Tillman" who completed it in 1470. Another huge figure of St Christopher by the same maestro is to be found in the fourth stained-glass window in the northern part of the nave. It however was done forty years later and shows St Christopher with the Baby Jesus on his shoulders crossing a river, much to the surprise of a monk who with lamp in hand is searching for God along the riverbank. Jesus looks with satisfaction on his labour and places his little hand on St Christopher's forehead as a gesture of comfort and blessing for the man who is taking him to the other side. The statue on the other hand shows St Christopher in a typical saintly pose which reminds us of how difficult it is for man to carry out the will of God. In general St Christopher stands near the church's main exit as a reminder to the visitor that while Christ appears benevolent within His church, once outside His expectations will put man to the test.

St Christopher (1470).

Angel with the coat-of-arms (1463) from the Sepulchre of Archbishop Dietrich von Moers

Stained-glass window in the Sakramentskapelle (second half of the 15th century): The Annunciation.   *Christ Before Pilate.*

Angel with the Coat-of-Arms
(from Archbishop Dietrich von Moers' Sepulchre)

The Cathedral is both the house of Our Lord and the archbishops' final resting place. The styles of the sepulchres vary greatly from very humble tombs to magnificently decorated ones. Behind the Casket of the Three Wise Men in front of the Dreikönigskapelle stands the *Sepulchre of Archbishop Dietrich von Moers* (1414-1443). It was built by the Cathedral's architect, Kuyn. In the centre stands Mary surrounded by two angels bearing a coat-of-arms. Mary points out the baby Jesus to the Three Wise Men who stand nearby. On her left St Peter introduces the archbishop on his bended knees to the child. The angel is holding the coat-of-arms of the archbishops of Cologne.

The Stained-Glass Windows from the Sakramentskapelle

The stained-glass windows of the Sakramentskapelle which also houses the Madonna of Milan were saved by Professor Wallraff during the time of the secularisation of the church. They consist of a series of 120 glass-plates. They belonged to the Convent of St Cecilia and were of the period prior to Stephen Lochner. In spite of the fact that they are not all the work of one man the influence of the master craftsman is still obvious especially in the ones dealing with Mary. In the left window starting from the bottom up is the *Annunciation*, the *Visitation*, the *Birth of Jesus* and then higher up the *Adoration of the Three Wise Men*, the *Presentation of Jesus at the Temple*, the *Flight into Egypt*, the *Slaughter of the Innocents* and concluding with *Scenes from Christ's Miracles*. The window on the right side depicts *Christ's Passion*. In the Annunciation scene the angel kneels before Mary, greeting her respectfully, while Mary caught in prayer turns fearfully towards him. Unlike Lochner's Annunciation the angel in this one inspires courage while Mary's expression reveals all her fears for the task that lies ahead of her. The lily on her kneeling-stool is a symbol of her virginity. The scenes from Christ's Passion are rich in detail. In the photo Pilate can be seen presenting Christ to the excited crowd. In Christ's face can be seen the suffering of all mankind while the angry crowd all around him clamours for his death. Pilate seems undecided while the spokesman for the crowd laughs triumphantly.

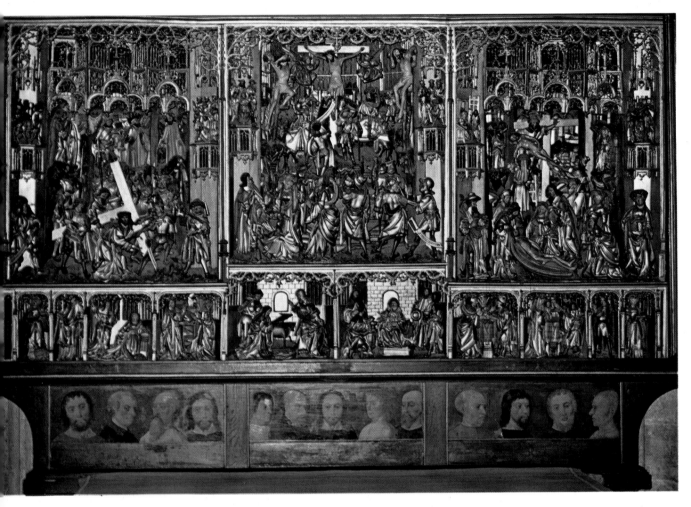

Altarpiece of St George in the
Engelbertkapelle (around 1520).

Altarpiece of the Crucifixion in the
Maternuskapelle (end of the 15th century).

The Altarpiece of St George

The *St Georgsaltar* (Altarpiece of
St George) in the Engelbert Chapel,
belongs to a group of works set
up in the Cathedral at the beginning of the nineteenth century. It
was placed in the Engelbertkapelle
behind Gero's Crucifix. It is a typical carved Flemish altarpiece, char-
acteristic of the Lower Rhine. It
was acquired for the Cathedral in
1840 by an art-dealer named
Gerling.

It tells with great drama and movement the *Story of the Passion*. In
the centre is the *Crucifixion*. In the
panel on the left Christ can be
seen carrying the Cross. He is
surrounded by his tormentors and
the crowd. The panel on the right
shows the *Deposition from the Cross*
and Mary and Christ's friends

mourning. The manner in which
the events are depicted make the
altarpiece a real drama in three
acts. Around the lower edge are
eight scenes depicting the *Story
of Christ's Childhood*. In the middle
ones are seen the *Adoration of the
Shepherds* and the *Adoration of
the Three Wise Men*. On the stand
is *Christ with His Twelve Apostles*.
Above the middle panel of this
large altarpiece (3.50m. long and
1.50m. high) is a carved polyptych.
In the centre can be seen the *Battle
between St George and the Dragon*
and in the side sections scenes
from *St George's Martyrdom*. In
spite of the fact that the altarpiece
relates the story of Christ's Passion
it takes its name from the panels
which were added later.

Even more dramatic than the St
George altarpiece and more impres-

sive (5.20m. high) is the Agilol-
phusaltar (the Agilulf Altarpiece)
in the southern transept of the Cathedral. It too was made in Ant-
werp, in 1520, for the church of
St Mary in Gradus which stood
behind the eastern part of the Cathedral's choir. When the church
was demolished the altarpiece was
transferred to the Cathedral in 1821.
It is the largest work of art to be
found inside the Cathedral, having
a length of 6.80m. Its panels are
admirable for their richness.

The Altarpiece of the Crucifixion
(in the Maternuskapelle)

From the same period but stylis-
tically different is the *Kreuzigungsaltar* (the Altarpiece of the Crucifixion) which comes from the Mid-
dle-Rhine region. It stands in the

Stephan Lochner: Altarpiece of the Patron Saints of the City, known as the « Altarpiece of the Cathedral ».

second chapel in the northern section of the choir. Our Lord's face is covered with blood and expresses great suffering. Mary and John stand at the foot of the Cross filled with grief and dismay. The side sections show *St John the Baptist* pointing to the lamb of God which awaits sacrifice and the first Christian martyrs, James the Elder, Stephen and Lawrence. The aim of this altarpiece as far as we

can tell from the pictures on the back was to give help and comfort to those suffering from epilepsy.

In the photo the towers on the corner of Archbishop Philipp von Heinsberg's sepulchre can be seen. He lived from 1167 to 1191. His tomb is surrounded by towers and crenellation as a reminder that during his time as archbishop the new city-walls were built extending its territory from 100 to 400 hectares.

The Cathedral Altarpiece by Stephen Lochner

At the end of the ambulatory in the Marienkapelle can be found one of the most important works donated to the Cathedral in the post-Napoleonic era. It is Stephen Lochner's *Altarpiece of the City's Patron Saints* or as it is known in German, "Dombild" (the Cathedral Altarpiece). It was painted by Loch-

« Altarpiece of the Cathedral »:
Entourage of St Ursula.

« Altarpiece of the Cathedral »:
Entourage of the King.

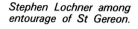

Stephen Lochner among
entourage of St Gereon.

ner before 1451 for the Town Hall chapel. It is a triptych in oak with an antique gilded frame. Its middle panel is 2.82m. high and 2.61m. wide while the side ones are 1.16m. wide. The triptych was brought to the Cathedral in 1804 and has been located in the southern section of the Marien-kapelle since 1950.

The name of the master, Stephen Lochner, had been forgotten for a long time. However it returned to prominence last century when Albrecht Dürer's diary of his travels in the Netherlands came to light. In his entry of October, 1520 he spoke of Lochner and his painting. There is a record of Lochner's presence in Cologne in 1442 when he was given little more than 40 shillings during the visit of Emperor Frederick III for having painted the festive decorations for his coronation at Aix-la-Chapelle. That same year he and his wife acquired a house. In 1447 he was granted citizenship and was a councillor up until 1448. He was reelected in 1451 but a cross appears after his name in the list of senators and it is possible he died during the plague which ravaged Cologne. A letter from the town-councillor of Cologne to his counterpart in Meersburg on Lake Constance in 1451 tells us he was born there.

Otto H. Foerster has written of the importance of Lochner's work for Cologne: "Nobody before Lochner so decisively influenced the art of Cologne. He came not so much as an innovator but as a breath of fresh air in a moment of need when the traditional local art seemed to have come to a standstill and threatened to disappear altogether." The painting was done for the chapel where the councillors took oath and where they met before making important decisions. The triptych's middle panel shows *Christ Seated on His Mother's Lap* surrounded by Cologne's *Patron Saints and the Three Wise Men.* The side panels depict *St Gereon and St Ursula.* The altarpiece was the spiritual symbol of the Town Hall and through it the citizens of Cologne paid homage to the Lord through the representations of their

« Altarpiece of the Cathedral »: St Ursula.

« Altarpiece of the Cathedral »: St Gereon.

patron saints in the heavenly court. This was much the same as occured in Northern Italy.

Christ is the centre of the work and, seated on Mary's lap, all light radiates from him. Seven incorporeal angels pay homage and at the same time invite the inhabitants of the city to fall in behind their patron saints to worship the Baby Jesus. The left panel of the triptych shows *St Ursula and the Virgins* in whose honour Cologne's coat-of-arms bears eleven flames. On the left panel *St Gereon* leads the citizens to defend their city. The grandiose style of the work is typical of Italian art while the minute attention to detail recalls Flemish painting. On close examination every head is worthy of a portrait while much care has also been taken with the flowers, ornaments and clothing. From this it may be assumed that the painter was also a fine goldsmith. He has included himself in the painting along with the men who are following

45

« Altarpiece of the Cathedral »: The Annunciation of Mary.

St Gereon: his slender right side is in sharp contrast to the mighty hilt of his sword as he places his left hand in wonder and respect on the shoulder of the young man who stands next to him. The whole spirit of the composition with its timeless golden background reminds us that Christmas is still the time for worshipping the Lord who is ever present with us.

The back part of the triptych is painted much more simply. It shows the *Annunciation* with the angel bringing Mary the good news. Mary with her lovely face and blonde hair, held by a double row of pearls, is kneeling in her room. Her hair falls down over her shoulders. Her room is neat and tidy, recalling how peaceful her life had been up until then. The large cape which lies at her feet seems to be a symbol of the disturbing and unforseen events which have unexpectedly disrupted her life. This dismay however is only momentary for with a movement of her left hand she gathers up the folds of her cape, as a sign that her faith and trust in God have won the day. Her hand is on the same plane as the three-flowered lily which seems to be opening towards God. On the vase are written the words: "Ecce ancilla Domini"(behold the handmaiden of the Lord). And like the lily Mary grew yearning for the Holy Trinity so she cannot but accept the angel's offer. And so begins the New Testament.

In front of Mary stands the angel whose powerful wings are a symbol of his heavenly origin. They seem to threaten to break asunder that earthly dwelling. Kneeling down the angel delivers his message: "Ave, gratia plena, Dominus tecum" (Hail Mary, full of grace, the Lord is with Thee). In his right hand he holds a sealed letter and in his left a heraldic staff, symbol of his heavenly mission. His cloak, red on the outside and green on the inside, is fastened by a clasp with the image of God. Above the golden border on both sides are three angels with their hands clasped in prayer. They stand out on a blue background. The part of the wings turned towards Mary is as light as day the other side as black as night. The beautiful face of the angel watches anxiously for the reactions of Mary who is the one chosen to rid the world of its eternal darkness by heralding in a new dawn. The Cathedral Altarpiece is one of the most admired works of art in the Cathedral today. Except for the winter months mass is celebrated daily in front of it. Its splendid colours inspire a deep and joyous reverence.

The Chasuble of the Passion

The Cathedral has many vestments of the sixteenth century which are still in use today. As the fabric was extremely worn, the threads have been sewn on to new material to preserve the garments. They reflect the taste of the times with their rich figurative decorations which speak highly of the skill of the craftswomen of their time.

The Chasuble of the Passion (16th century).

The Adoration of the Shepherds
(third northern window)

The five magnificent stained-glass windows in the northern aisle belong to the Renaissance period and are witness to the high level of expertise of the glass industry at that time. They are the work of the most important school of painters from the end of the fifteenth century to the beginning of the sixteenth. The three middle ones are the work of the Master of the Holy Family who was in Cologne from 1486 to 1515 and of the Master of St Severin who was active from 1480 to 1520.

The central window in the northern aisle was donated to the Cathedral by the city of Cologne in 1507. In the upper half can be seen the *Adoration of the Shepherds*. They are on their way to the manger. Inside are Joseph, Mary and the Baby Jesus. Other angels are flying round the rafters and on closer inspection a host of them can be seen praising the Lord in joyous wonder. Kneeling round the Christ child in place of the usual cherubs is a group of distinguished figures. From their clothing it may well be that they are the town councillors come to pay homage to the Lord.

The Flagellation

From the first half of the stained-glass windows in the northern aisle.

The first stained-glass window in the northern aisle tells in the three double glass panels of the upper section the *Story of Christ's Passion* from the *Mount of Olives*, the *Mockery*, the *Flagellation*, the *Ecce Homo*, the *Crucifixion* and ends with the *Resurrection*.

The Beginning of the Manuscript with the Annunciation
(Cod. 274., 1531)

In the sixteenth century not only did the art of the embroidery of sacred vestments flourish but also that of illuminated manuscripts which developed mainly in the Convent of the Brothers of St Michael who lived according to the principles of Devotio Moderna as expounded

Third stained-glass window in the northern aisle (1507): The Adoration of the Shepherds.

First half of the stained-glass window on the northern side (1509): The Flagellation.

in the "Imitation of Christ" by Thomas von Kempen. They strove for a more fervid devotion to Christ through the study of texts and contemplation. The Cathedral's library contains many hymn books from their school. The *Manuscript 274* is a gradual 51cm. by 37cm. consisting of 278 thick parchment pages. It was used by the choirboys as a hymn book to sing the solemn mass. Today it can be found in the Cathedral's Treasury.

Mary and Joseph
(Evangelistary Manuscript 14, p. 15, ninth century)

Also in the Cathedral's Treasury can be found *Manuscript 14,* an evangelistary of the ninth century around the time when Hildebold built the Carolingian Cathedral and established the library.

The photo shows an excerpt from the beginning of the Gospel according to St Matthew. Mary and Joseph are setting out to follow the will of God.

Just as their journey was long and tortuous so too was the building of the Cathedral. The stained-glass windows in the northern section record the burning desire of the citizens of Cologne in the sixteenth century to complete the building. The pillars and the outside walls with their seven vaults in the western section were as yet unfinished. Philipp von Daun, Canon, and therefore administrator of the Cathedral's wealth was archbishop from 1508 to 1515 and he pledged himself to seeing that work on the Cathedral went ahead. The two stained-glass windows he ordered testify to this. In 1559 however all building activity came to a standstill and for 280 years the crane suspended in mid-air symbolised the grand undertaking which because of the turmoil of the times was unable to be brought to fruition. Besides, the Renaissance with its new concept of man as the measure of all things had no time for a temple that towered into the sky.

Manuscript 274 (1531):
The Annunciation of Mary.

Manuscript 14 (9th century):
Mary and Joseph.

INTERLUDE

Engelbert's Casket.

Work on the Cathedral stopped in 1560 and did not begin again until 1842. Clemente Augustus, one of the five Wittelsbachs who were archbishops and prince electors in Cologne from 1583 to 1761, took as active interest in the Cathedral and from 1735 to 1751 had important construction work carried out aimed mainly at consolidating the existing building. In 1660 the prince elector Maximillian Henry ordered the building of a Baroque-style *Mausoleum to the Three Wise Men* to decorate the inside of the Cathedral. The front part of the mausoleum was used as an altar in 1920 in the northern section of the transept where today can be found the small, richly adorned Madonna. In 1683 the Altarpiece of the Crucifixion was made to stand under Gero's Crucifix. In 1767 the high altar was made Baroque and in 1770 the eastern part of the choir. The iron-gates are a reminder of this period. Precious vestments were ordered like those in the "Clementina Chapel" which Archbishop Augustus had made in Lyons in 1742 for the coronation of his brother Charles VII. Many of these vestments can be seen in the Treasury and are still worn today to celebrate mass.

The Treasury also contains the *Engelbertschrein* (Engelbert's Casket). Engelbert was an archbishop assassinated in 1225. The casket was completed in 1633 by the master, Konrad Duisbergh. The figures cast in silver are the work of the sculptor, Jeremias Geisselbrunn who was also responsible for the statue of Hubert to be found in the Marienkapelle and the Apostles in the church of Mariä-Himmelfahrt. In the foreground is a portrait of *Christ Between Peter and Maternus* and in the background the *Three Wise Men Paying Homage to Mary*. On the sides are

Engelbert's Casket (1633).

shown the *Ten Holy Bishops of Cologne* gathered round their predecessor, Maternus. On the lid lies the body of Engelbert. Sixteen silver, bas-relief figures show the *Life and Work of the Saint* according to Caesarius von Heisterbach's version given not long after the saint's death. The four Evangelists who surround the saint are witness to his work.

The Cathedral's Ostensory

Another masterpiece by the goldsmiths of Cologne is the precious ostensory of pure gold and precious stones made in 1657 by Christus Schweling. It is evidence of the close ties that existed between Cologne and Augusta. The ostensory was given to the Cathedral by Archbishop Max Heinrich von Wittelsbach (1650-1688). Both crowns were donated by F. E. von Fürstenberg who was minister of Cologne up until 1663. One of the most spectacular jewel robberies of our time involved the theft of the ostensory. On a stormy night on 2nd November 1975 thieves entered the Treasury through the ventilator. There were alarms everywhere except, of course, there. The thieves had carefully planned the robbery and stole only the most valuable objects. Their choice had been facilitated by an exhibition at the Rheinisches Landesmuseum in Bonn from 16th February till 2nd March 1975 the catalogue of which listed all the Renaissance and Baroque works by the Rheinish goldsmiths. In the course of the robbery one of the thieves had inadvertently knocked over an ostensory and it fell to the ground. The noise attracted the attention of the guards but because of the thunder they were unable to tell where it came from. They searched the whole Cathedral before opening the Treasury. This gave the thieves plenty of time to make good their escape so that at first the police hunt had little success.

Then with the help of Interpol two of the thieves were arrested in Switzerland and part of the stolen goods was recovered. However the gold from the ostensory had already been melted down by a dentist. Of course it is irreplaceable but at the moment a copy is being made by Peter Bolg and it will be a reminder of this robbery for a long time to come, just as the famous *Cameo of Ptolemy* (247 B. C.) in Vienna brings to mind the theft of the Casket of the Three Wise Men in 1574.

"The Ostensory of the Cathedral" (1657).

Rubens' Tapestries

Rubens' tapestries were the second gift given to the Cathedral in 1687 by Franz Egon von Fürstenberg who had in the meantime become the prince bishop of Strasbourg and a cardinal. Thanks to the tapestries which were hung on the dividing-walls of the choir-stalls the 13th century frescos were spared attempts at up-dating and were preserved intact until 1842 when the tapestries were removed. The tapestries were made in the workshop of Franz van den Hecke in Brussels. The drawings were done by Rubens in 1627 for the Infante Isabella of Spain who had commissioned the work for the Convent of the Carmelites in Madrid. The tapestries show the *Triumph of the Eucharist and the Faith*. Today they can be seen in the nave of the Cathedral during the Corpus Christi celebrations. In 1977 it was possible to see the tapestries in normal lighting conditions at the "Exhibition of Rubens' Jubilee" in the Kunsthalle of Cologne. In the photos details can be seen of the *Sacrifice of the Old Testament* (4 × 6.65m.) and the *Meeting of Abraham and Melchizedek* (4.20 × 6.55m.). The bloody sacrifice of the lambs in the temple of Jerusalem, as told in the Old Testament, ended with the sacrifice of Christ on the cross which in Holy Communion is symbolised by the taking of the bread and the wine.

Rubens' Tapestries (1627): The Sacrifice of the Old Testament.

Rubens' Tapestries (1627): the Meeting of Abraham and Melchizedek.

The Madonna of Mercy (18th century).

The Madonna of Mercy

Today the little Madonna of Mercy in rococo style is found in the northern part of the transept where from 1920 to 1930 the Casket of the Three Wise Men was located. Every morning candles are lit in front of the Madonna of Mercy by people who come to pray on their way to work. Their religious fervour is deep, if a little naive. The small statue is wrapped in a cape which covers the Baby Jesus.

Mary is depicted as the queen of Heaven and stands on a crescent. Her left hand is outstretched to hold a sceptre (which has been lost), while in her right she cradles the Child who holds a globe of the world in his hand. It is amazing to see so large a cape enfold such a small statue only 70cm. high. The burned-out candles, the many strands of pearls and other objects of greater or lesser value are proof of the esteem in which the Madonna of Mercy is held by those who come to pray.

Ansicht des Domplatzes zu Kölln Vue de la place du Dôme à Cologne

Drawing by Janscha-Ziegler

The drawing by Janscha-Ziegler shows the southern part of the Cathedral as seen by a visitor in 1798. In the large building on the right was the priests' seminary which by that time was no longer used as such. It was not until 1824 that it came back into use as a seminary. In fact it was outgrown just four years after its completion because of the great influx of seminarians. As a result the seminary was moved to the one-time Convent of the Gesuits in the Marzellenstraße which is today the headquarters of the General Vicariate. The parish church of St John the Evangelist which stood next door was used as the seminary chapel but was demolished in 1829. The buttresses (completed in 1322) of the Cathedral's choir dominate the whole city and the square below. The crane for many years the city's symbol, but after 1560 no longer in use, can be seen overhanging the southern tower of which only three floors are completed. The Cathedral remained the way Janscha-Ziegler had designed it until 1840 when the plans for the continuation of its construction were ready and work could begin once more.

THE COMPLETION OF THE CATHEDRAL IN THE NINETEENTH CENTURY

The transformation of the eastern part of the choir to a Baroque design was the last major work carried out on the Cathedral. The French Revolution with its motto of "Liberty, Equality and Fraternity" deranged men's minds so that war was inevitable. In 1794 the victorious revolutionary troops entered Cologne and religious freedom ceased to exist. "Reason" triumphed to later flounder. Nevertheless in the future the dream of a new Cathedral fired the hearts of many. Fortunately Wallraff had managed to save many of the Cathedral's masterpieces from destruction. Men like Goethe, Görres and Schlegel rallied to the cause. The keenest however were the Boisserée brothers who published the plans for the reconstruction of the Cathedral. Part of this material turned up by chance in 1814 in a tavern, the "Zur Traube", at Darmstadt. A large parchment sheet was found in a long forgotten trunk tucked away in the corner of the attic. The drawing was identified by the director of Fine Arts at Assia as the old plan for the façade of the Cathedral of Cologne. Two years later another two similar drawings were found in the National Library in Paris. In 1814 S. Boisserée had spoken to Frederick William about his plans for the Cathedral and the prince had been most enthusiastic. When he became King of Prussia in 1840 things began to move and by 1842 work had begun. The architects, Ernst Zwirner and Richard Voigtel, managed to complete it in 38 years. In 1863 the western part which had kept the choir closed for more

The towers of the Cathedral.

The spire of a tower seen from the inside.

Inside view of the Cathedral.

The Stained-Glass Window of the Pentecost.

In the spandrels: Angels.

than 550 years was finally demolished. On 14th October 1880 the last stone was placed on the towers. The Cathedral, the symbol of one great faith for over six centuries was finally completed.

On entering the Cathedral the visitor is struck above all by its vastness. He is unconciously aware of its harmony without realising that it derives from the laws of proportion which were already known in ancient times and were used by the Cathedral's architects to create a new concept in architecture. Anyone who tried to measure it in human terms would give up immediately. Its pillars which soar towards heaven are almost 44m. high and support the weight of the vaults which reach out into space and give the Cathedral the appearance of a great tent. The weight of the building goes unnoticed and its space seems limitless. The brightness of the stained-glass windows seems to put us in touch with the world of redemption they portray. The statues on the pillars entice us to follow their long line. It must be understood that the Cathedral is the work of the human mind and its great will power and as well a work of love. It invites man to serve God and seek enlightenment as those who came before him. did. He who enters the Cathedral must try to come to terms with himself and then and only then will he be able to understand how insignificant he is and yet at the same time of great importance in the eyes of the Lord.

The next thing which attracts the visitor's gaze are the stained-glass windows on the southern side of the Cathedral. They were donated by Ludwig I of Bavaria and installed in 1848. In the centre of each of the three windows can be seen scenes from Mary's life, *Mary on Christmas Night, Mary at the foot of the Cross* and *Mary with the faithful at Pentecost.*

The half-windows depict scenes from the *Life of St John, the Baptist* who paved the way for Christ, and *St Stephen, the first Christian Martyr*. The Pentecost Window and that of St Stephen are still to be found in the southern part of the transept but it is hoped that one day they will be returned to their original position.

The statues on the pillars by P. Fuchs, C. Mohr and A. Werres, seem to be reminding us that the saints are the spiritual columns of the church. The sculptures on the pillars at the centre of the crossing show the *Four Evangelists,* the four great doctors of the Western church, while the sculptures on on the pillars in the transept depict the *Four Great Teachers of the Eastern Church*. The remaining statues record the various facets of the church's work over the centuries: teaching, charity and religious rites.

Further work was also undertaken on the choir. A rich *mosaic floor* by Jennewein shows the *Hierarchy of Earthly Order* and in the spandrels of the arches paintings by E. von Steinle from 1843 to 1845 shown the *Captains of the Heavenly Angels* with archangels and angels gathered round the throne in prayer.

Statue on a pillar:
Pope Gregory Magne.

Northern side of the choir.

Two Pastoral Staffs

Whereas the choir had been consecrated in 1322 it was not until 1880 that the Cathedral itself was ready for consecration. The Christian faith had remained unchanged for all those years! This can also be seen in the decoration of pastoral staffs from the years 1350 and 1893. The first shows Archbishop Wilhelm von Gennep on bended knee in front of the enthroned Madonna who is holding Baby Jesus out towards him. On the curve of the staff is an angel who holds up the scene. The pastoral staff is gold and has brightly coloured enamel work which enhances its beauty. The second staff is very similar in form to the first one. It belonged to the auxiliary bishop, Hermann-Josef Schmitz, formerly from the parish of Essen, who brought the staff with him to Cologne. On this one instead of the bishop kneeling in prayer in front of the Christ Child it shows him in the act of offering Jesus an apple, just as his patron saint, Hermann-Josef, was supposed to have done in the church of Santa Maria in Campidoglio. By offering the apple the bishop gives up all his worldly goods. His staff becomes the symbol of his office which requires self-denial and self-sacrifice. Here too an angel supports the decoration on the crook. The coat-of-arms of the city of Essen is a reminder of the bishop's origin. Even if 632 years had passed from the founding of the Gothic Cathedral to its completion the spirit of its bishops, priests and the faithful remained as steadfast as ever. The Cathedral whose towers soar above the city like hands folded in prayer welcomes people from all walks of life to lift up their hearts towards God, forget their differences and live in the joy of the faith.

Pastoral Staff (1350).

Pastoral Staff (1893).

THE THIRD PERIOD OF CONSTRUCTION

After its completion the Cathedral remained intact for only a short time. In 1904 the architect, Hertel established a workshop to repair damage to the Cathedral caused by the elements. In addition the buttresses in the choir had to be restored. Work also went ahead on the decoration of the inside of the Cathedral. The plan by Essenwein for a mosaic floor in the choir and the ambulatory went ahead. The floor with its religious symbols was laid down between 1892 and 1897. Even after its completion the Cathedral continued to bear witness to the creativity of the greatest artists of their time!

The First World War passed without any serious damage to the Cathedral. The Second World War however caused extensive damage to the great building. Although the great powers involved in the conflict did their best to save the famous building the toll was nevertheless heavy. The ten roofs over the vaults in the nave and the northern part of the transept and four of those over the aisles were damaged by bombing. The roof over the northern part of the transept was destroyed and the northern part of the buttresses on the western façade was torn apart. The bricks on the façade and the scaffolding on the northern part record to this day the havoc wrought by the war. In the time of the Third Reich the faithful gathered in the Cathedral for solemn masses and sermons. The number of people present ranged from 10,000 to 20,000 but the press made no mention of it. On occasion of the consecration of

Series of Frescos: Angel.

The Magnificat.

Cardinal Frings to bishop on 21st June 1942 20,000 people were present. The only mention of it in the press was a brief notice about a young woman who had lost her purse at the ceremony and begged anyone who had found it to return the photo of her fiancé who was away at the front.

On 15th August, 1948, the 700th anniversary of the founding of the Cathedral, Archbishop Frings invited the faithful to celebrate this important occasion. It was a day of universal reconcilement. Pope Pius XII sent Cardinal Micara, the oldest bishop from the Roman curia as his representative; there were eight cardinals, including those from Paris, London, Holland and Belgium and many bishops from all over the world. They filed in procession behind the Casket of the Three Wise Men through the piles of rubble to the Cathedral, where the choir had been prepared for the occasion. They made it known that with their coming peace would prevail. By 1956 on the occasion of the German Catholics' National Convention the whole of the Cathedral was once more in use.

Today work is still proceeding in a permanent workshop where experts are fighting a continuing battle against the ravages of wind, inclement weather and above all exhaust fumes from cars and air pollution. The architect, A. Wolff who took over from W. Weyres in 1972, and his sixty assistants are fighting a battle with time.

During the war the choir, too, was destroyed. In 1948 W. Weyres built a new one on two pillars of cement. Then in 1964 on the 800th anniversary of the transfer to Cologne of the bones of the Three Wise Men, Peter Hecker painted a grandiose series of frescos below the choir. They show the *Adoration of the Lamb* with characters from the Old and the New Testaments praising God with singing and music. Among these are the archangels, the conductors of the heavenly choir. Behind the angels can be seen a line of men who distinguished themselves by rescu-

Bronze doors at the southern entrance to the Cathedral.

The Cathedral, southern door.

Side door: the Cathedral amidst the city in flames.

ing Cologne and the Cathedral in time of war. At their feet lies the city spread out around the Rhine. The other fresco in the photo is found at the entrance to the archbishops' crypt. It shows Mary, Mother of God, singing the Magnificat while at her feet Peter Hecher has drawn the small figure of the Archbishop Cardinal of Cologne who was blind praising the Lord with his violin.

In 1948 E. Mataré made the Bronze Doors for the southern entrance to the Cathedral on occasion of its jubilee. On the upper panels can be seen the coats-of-arms of Pope Pius XII and Archbishop Cardinal Frings; below them are the seven saints of Cologne symbols of the seven gifts of the Holy Spirit. Underneath the coat-of-arms of the Pope, Mataré has put a rooster and a pelican in brightly coloured mosaic as symbols of vigilance and love. A plate in the door on the left side shows the city in flames with the Cathedral in its midst.

In front of the plaque showing the Cathedral near the main door E. Mataré made a fountain for the pigeons. It is decorated with beautiful mosaics and is a favourite spot for children playing and elderly people seeking a little peace and quiet. The water flows along a spiral course and through a gutter-pipe from which the pigeons can drink with ease. Sometimes the Cathedral is reflected in the fountain and the circles of the spiral distort its image. It is then that the visitor who has lingered there musing may recall the verses from Rilke's first *Book of Gold:*

"*I live my life*
in concentric circles
that spread out ever more.
I may not complete the last one,
but at least I want to try.
I revolve round God,
round the most ancient towers,
and I have been turning and turning
                    [*for millenniums,*
and I do not know for how much
                    [*longer*
I will be a hawk, a tempest
or a great poem."

The Pigeon Fountain.